BLACK GIRL

coloring book for adults

Thank You!

As the author of this coloring book, I wanted to take a moment to express our heartfelt gratitude for choosing our book and completing this incredible journey. It brings us great joy to know that our small, company has been a part of your life.

If you enjoyed this coloring book and found it to be a source of joy, encouragement, and growth, we kindly invite you to leave a review on Amazon. Your words carry immense power and can make a significant impact on our small business. Your support will not only help us reach more people but also inspire us to continue creating meaningful books.

We understand that leaving a review may seem like a small action, but to us, it means the world. Your support will enable us to continue producing quality books that touch the lives of people and nourish their imaginations.

With deep appreciation,
Rosemary Wilcher

Contact us!

It is important for us to let you know that we appreciate any feedback on our creations and if you have any suggestions for improvement, you can contact us at our email address:

paloverose@gmail.com

With deep appreciation,

Rosemary Wilcher

BLACK girls are magic

BLACK girls are magic

BLACK girls are magic

BLACK girls are magic

BLACK girls are magic

BLACK girls are magic

BLACK girls are magic

BLACK girls are magic

BLACK girls are magic

BLACK girls are magic

BLACK girls are magic

BLACK girls are magic

BLACK girls are magic

BLACK girls are magic

BLACK girls are magic

BLACK girls are magic

BLACK girls are magic

BLACK girls are magic

BLACK girls are magic

BLACK girls are magic

BLACK girls are magic

BLACK girls are magic

BLACK girls are magic

BLACK girls are magic

BLACK girls are magic

BLACK
girls
are
magic

BLACK girls are magic

BLACK girls are magic

BLACK girls are magic

BLACK girls are magic

BLACK girls are magic

BLACK girls are magic

BLACK girls are magic

BLACK girls are magic

BLACK girls are magic

BLACK girls are magic

BLACK girls are magic

BLACK girls are magic

BLACK girls are magic

BLACK girls are magic

BLACK girls are magic

BLACK girls are magic

BLACK girls are magic

BLACK girls are magic

BLACK girls are magic

BLACK girls are magic

BLACK
girls
are
magic

BLACK
girls
are
magic

BLACK girls are magic

BLACK girls are magic